THE *U.S. Congress*

Our Government and Citizenship

SPIRIT
of America®

THE *U.S. Congress*

By Kevin Cunningham

*Content Adviser: David R. Smith, PhD, Academic Advisor and Adjunct
Assistant Professor of History, The University of Michigan, Ann Arbor, Michigan*

*The Child's World
Chanhassen, Minnesota*

THE *U.S. Congress*

Published in the United States of America by The Child's World®
PO Box 326 • Chanhassen, MN 55317-0326 • 800-599-READ • www.childsworld.com

Acknowledgments
    The Child's World®: Mary Berendes, Publishing Director

    Editorial Directions, Inc.: E. Russell Primm, Editorial Director; Pam Rosenberg, Line Editor; Katie
    Marsico, Associate Editor; Judi Shiffer, Associate Editor and Library Media Specialist; Matthew
    Messbarger, Editorial Assistant; Susan Hindman, Copy Editor; Lucia Raatma, Proofreader; Judith
    Frisbee, Peter Garnham, and Olivia Nellums, Fact Checkers; Tim Griffin/IndexServ, Indexer; Cian
    Loughlin O'Day, Photo Researcher; Linda S. Koutris, Photo Selector

Photo
    Cover/frontispiece: Joseph Sohm; ChromoSohm Inc./Corbis.
    Interior: AP/Wide World: 13 (J. Scott Applewhite), 22 (Reed Saxon); Bettmann/Corbis: 12, 17, 23;
    Corbis: 7 (Lester Lefkowitz), 11 (Richard Bickel), 16 (Philip Gould), 18 (Wally McNamee), 26 (Ron
    Sachs/CNP), 28 (Hulton-Deutsch Collection); Getty Images: 9 (Hulton|Archive), 10 (AFP/Stephen
    Jaffe), 24 (William Thomas Cain); Getty Images/Newsmakers: 14 (Alex Wong), 20 (Mark Wilson).

Registration

Library of Congress Cataloging-in-Publication Data
    Cunningham, Kevin, 1966–
    The U.S. Congress : who represents you / by Kevin Cunningham.
        p. cm. — (Our government and citizenship)
    Includes index.
    ISBN 1-59296-327-7 (library bound : alk. paper) 1. United States. Congress—History—Juvenile
literature. 2. Legislators—United States—History—Juvenile literature. I. Title. II.
Series.
    JK1025.C86 2005
    328.73—dc22   2004007200

Contents

Creating Congress

CONGRESS IS THE **LEGISLATURE** OF THE UNITED States government. The men and women who serve in Congress share a staggering responsibility. They're in charge of passing laws in every area of American society, from real estate to health care. Congress also decides how to spend the trillions of dollars the government collects in taxes and other **revenues.**

Despite holding all this power, every member of Congress must answer to his or her **constituents.** There can be a lot to answer for. Voters push to make new laws, get rid of old laws, or send more money to their city or state. Make enough of the constituents unhappy, and a congressperson will need to find a new job.

The people who wrote the U.S. **Constitution** wanted a system that answered to the people. The question was, How much answering did they want their leaders to do?

On May 25, 1787, **delegates** from 12 states gathered at a meeting in Philadelphia, Pennsylvania, to discuss a constitution for a new American government. One historian summed up the participants as "the well-bred, the well-fed, the well-read, and the well-wed." Many of the richest men in the colonies attended this meeting. Famous figures such as Benjamin Franklin, Alexander Hamilton, James Madison, and George Washington were also there.

Throughout the summer of 1787, the delegates hashed out a new constitution. The delegates argued and discussed for weeks on end, as they worked on a document critical to the survival of the country. The delegates drew on their immense knowledge of law

The delegates to the Constitutional Convention met in this room in Independence Hall.

7

and history. They also drew on recent ideas. One of those was that any good government must have the "the consent of the governed."

Some delegates felt elected officials should do what the voters wanted, without much freedom to make their own choices. Others disagreed. They believed that elected officials had to be more than just tools of the voters. Otherwise, nothing would get done.

The delegates also argued about how much **democracy** to allow. When it came down to it, many of the delegates liked the idea of democracy more than the actual practice of democracy. The people deserved to give their approval, but they weren't perfect. They might make serious mistakes because of fear, anger, or bad leaders. Handing the voters total control of government could lead to disaster.

In part, these worries led the delegates to adopt a bicameral legislature. This means it is divided into two houses, the House of Representatives and the Senate. The members of the House of Representatives would be elected directly by the people. This gave voters an important voice in getting new laws passed. A second group—the Senate—would coolly study legislation passed by the House. Members of the Senate would be chosen by state legislatures, not by voters. This wasn't exactly the democracy many Americans had fought for. Some of them said so. But the delegates at this meeting, right or wrong, considered it vital to strike a balance between the House and the Senate.

The delegates also faced the problem of how to divide up the seats in Congress. Large states with lots of people, such as New York and Virginia, wanted the number of congressmen from each state to be based on the population of that state. Small states worried that this would leave them with no power. They wanted every state to have the same number of representatives. The fight was long and bitter. Many people, including George Washington, feared it might never be settled.

Roger Sherman, a delegate from Connecticut, came up with a **compromise.** In the House, the number of representatives from each state would be based on population. In the Senate, each state would get two senators. Because both the House and the Senate have to pass new laws, neither large nor small states would have an advantage.

This solution created another problem. How should people held as slaves be counted? In the northern states, slavery was rare. Northern delegates thought that slaves should not be counted as part of the population. But in the South, slavery was common. Southern delegates thought slaves should be counted, despite the fact that slaves could not vote

Roger Sherman was born in Newton, Massachusetts, in 1721. He served in Congress as a representative from 1789–1791 and as a senator from 1791–1793.

President George W. Bush addresses a joint session of Congress. The delegates to the Constitutional Convention created the bicameral legislature that has been in existence for over 200 years.

or own property and were not taxed. Counting slaves would give southern states more representatives in the House. Under a second compromise, each slave counted as three-fifths of a person.

Finally, the delegates in Philadelphia had devised a government for the United States. It would have three branches: a legislature to make laws (the legislative branch), a court system to decide whether the laws obey the Constitution (the judicial branch), and a president who has the power to **veto** any law (the executive branch). This system keeps any one part of government from becoming too powerful.

Yet the delegates seemed to think that Congress was the most important branch, for they discussed it first—before the president, before the courts. Congress is described in the very first section of the Constitution.

THE U.S. CONSTITUTION GAVE CONGRESS MANY POWERS. SOME OF THEM involved setting up the early government of the United States. Others are the basic powers that Congress has to this day. According to the Constitution, Congress has the power to:

- Require and collect taxes and other kinds of revenue
- Provide money to defend the country
- Borrow money and pay debts
- Make rules for trade with other nations
- Create laws for citizenship and bankruptcy
- Issue money
- Create a post office
- Create copyright and patent laws
- Establish a court system below the Supreme Court
- Define and punish piracy and other crimes committed at sea
- Declare war
- Raise and support armed forces, and make rules for their use
- Create an armed militia and call them out in case of rebellion or invasion
- Govern and create rules for a capital city
- Make any other laws necessary

Chapter TWO

The House of Representatives

Women march in a parade for woman suffrage in New York City in 1915.

FROM THE TIME THE CONSTITUTION WAS WRITTEN, voters have directly elected their representatives to the House. But for much of the country's history, "voters" did not mean all Americans. When the Constitution was written, people had to pass three tests to be able to vote:

They had to be male.

They had to be white.

They had to own property.

All of that has changed, of course. Laws requiring that a voter own property went out by the middle of the 19th century. The Fifteenth **Amendment** said states could not prohibit people from voting because of their race. It went into effect in 1870. And the Nineteenth Amendment guaranteed women the right to vote in 1920.

Both houses of Congress have been meeting in the U.S. Capitol in Washington, D.C., since 1800. Before that time, Philadelphia, Pennsylvania, served as the capital of the United States.

Representatives are elected to two-year terms. The people who devised the Constitution wanted to make sure the representatives actually represented the voters' beliefs and interests. Having only two-year terms gave voters plenty of chances to replace these leaders.

There are 435 members of the House of Representatives. Each House member represents about 600,000 people in a district. Some districts have fewer people, however. This is because the Constitution says that every state gets at least one representative. And some states such as Wyoming have fewer than 600,000 people.

Every 10 years, the U.S. government performs a census, or count, of all the people in the country. The

Interesting Fact

▸ In 1870, Republican minister Hiram Revels of Mississippi became the first African-American elected to the Senate. He served for one year. In 1992, Illinois's Carol Mosley Braun became the first African-American woman elected to the Senate.

▶ There are 435 full members in the House of Representatives. In addition, the House includes a few delegates from U.S. lands around the world, including Guam, American Samoa, and the District of Columbia. Puerto Rico's delegate to the house is called the resident commissioner. These delegates vote on **committees,** but not as part of the House as a whole.

census determines the number of seats for each state. State legislatures draw new maps of the districts in their state after each census is finished. New boundaries mean changes. A House member may gain new constituents. If so, he or she will need to learn their wants and needs—and fast. In a state that loses a seat, the representative is suddenly out of a job. He or she will either retire or run for a seat in a new district.

Power in the House tilts heavily toward the **majority** party, these days either Democrats or

Illinois representative Dennis Hastert was sworn in as Speaker of the House in January 1999.

14

Republicans. The party with the most seats elects the Speaker of the House and the majority leader. These two powerful representatives control which bills are considered and voted on. Politics in the House tends to be rough. The majority party is often unwilling to compromise.

Most of a representative's work takes place in committees. Each committee specializes in a different area. These include issues such as the environment, taxes, education, and relations with foreign countries. Committees have many responsibilities. They gather information about the areas they oversee, and they write laws.

A good committee assignment is very important to the career of a representative. A House member can ask to be on certain committees, but the party leaders decide. Not everyone gets to be on the committees they want, especially if they haven't been in the House very long.

The majority party has more members on each committee and elects its leader. The head of the committee is called the chairman or chairwoman. The leader from the minority party on each committee is called its ranking member. A representative who holds one of these powerful positions can get a lot done for his district.

Getting things done is the name of the game in politics. This might mean getting money for a new

Interesting Fact

▶ Members, of Congress, especially those in the House, do a lot of favors for their constituents. They may help constituents get government benefits, write a letter on their behalf, or lend a hand in another way. These efforts are called casework.

15

highway or school. It might mean a vote for important legislation that's been in the news. When representatives can point to such accomplishments, people are more likely to give them money and votes. And it takes lots of both to win elections.

This makes it sound as if only those who do a good job get reelected. That is not really the case. For years, voters have been losing interest in House elections. Polls show more than half of all Americans don't know who their representatives are. More than 90 percent of those running for reelection win. In fact, it's only news when someone loses.

Congressman William J. Jefferson of Louisiana greets one of his constituents.

REDRAWING DISTRICT BOUNDARIES AFTER THE CENSUS OFTEN LEADS TO BIG battles between Democrats and Republicans. Each side tries to draw the map so that their party has the most seats. Often boundaries hook and turn so weirdly they look like they've been drawn with an Etch-A-Sketch.

Drawing such a map is called gerrymandering. Gerrymandering is an old tradition in American politics. The word comes from the name of Elbridge Gerry (below), a signer of the Declaration of Independence, governor of Massachusetts, and fifth vice president of the United States.

After the census of 1810, Massachusetts redrew its district boundaries. The party that controlled the Massachusetts legislature at the time was called the Democratic-Republicans. They got to redraw the boundaries.

New districts with Democratic-Republican majorities wound all over the place. At the same time, areas supporting the other party, the Federalists, were reduced to a small number of districts. Governor Gerry, a Democratic-Republican, approved the new map.

The story goes that a reporter at a Federalist paper showed the map to his editor. One of the new Democratic-Republican districts twisted so much, he said, that it looked like a salamander. His outraged editor exclaimed, "Salamander! Call it a Gerrymander!"

Soon after, the word *gerrymander*—the act of redrawing district boundaries to give one party an advantage over the other—entered the language.

Chapter THREE

The Senate

THE CONSTITUTION GIVES EACH STATE—FROM TINY Rhode Island to big California—a pair of senators. Senators are elected every six years. This gives senators time to learn about issues and discuss new **legislation,** without having to worry so much about what the voters back home think. For much of U.S. history, state legislatures elected senators. But in

U.S. senators at work in the Senate chamber.

1913, the Seventeenth Amendment changed the Constitution by allowing the voters of each state to elect U.S. senators.

The U.S. Senate considers laws sent to it by the House. It has the power to approve, change, or ignore those laws. Legislation can also start in the Senate. It must pass both houses of Congress before being sent on to the president.

Voters expect their senators to see that legislation helps their home state. That can mean paying for a project that brings jobs. It could also mean getting money to rebuild after a hurricane. Stopping legislation that could hurt the state is just as important. An example of this might be blocking a nuclear waste dump from being built in their state.

When considering new laws, the Senate focuses on issues important to the whole country. This includes debating vital national concerns, such as taxes or the military. It also means dealing with social issues such as health insurance or guns.

The Senate has duties beyond making new laws. It approves or blocks treaties, or agreements, with other nations. The Senate also approves the president's choices for many important jobs. These jobs include justices of the Supreme Court, ambassadors, or representatives, to foreign countries, and some of the president's top advisers. Most of these appointments get approved without much of a problem, but a few spark intense emotions and

19

The Senate Judiciary Committee at work during confirmation hearings for Attorney General John Ashcroft.

strong debate. In these cases, a senator must balance his own beliefs with the knowledge that constituents will remember how he voted. Such emotional issues can cause a senator a lot of trouble come election time.

The Senate moves slowly. Because senators serve six-year terms, they have time to work together and get to know one another. The tradition of cooperation is very strong, and the Senate is considered friendlier than the House. Senate rules give the minority party much more of a chance to make changes to laws.

The top position in the Senate is called the president of the Senate. This is not as important as it sounds. Officially, the vice president of the

United States is president of the Senate, but he rarely attends except when there is a tie vote. When that happens, the vice president gets a vote to break the tie.

The Senate's real boss is the majority leader. As in the House, this is the leader of whichever party holds the most seats. The majority leader controls the Senate schedule. This is a very powerful job, because it determines which bills are voted on and which aren't. The other party elects a minority leader to act as its spokesman.

Committees play an important role in the Senate. In committee, senators judge whether or not legislation should be passed. They might make changes to a bill or decide how much money a program should get. Sometimes a senator adds on his own legislation to a bill. Often this extra legislation has nothing to do with the original bill. It's allowed to ride along in return for the senator's vote.

All committees handle important legislation. One that gets a lot of attention is the Appropriations Committee, which determines how much money is given to government programs. Another is the Ways and Means Committee, which handles tax policy and big programs such as Social Security. The Budget Committee also deals with tax policy and how much the government borrows and spends.

▸ In 1932, Democrat Hattie Ophelia Wyatt Caraway of Arkansas became the first woman elected to the Senate.

California firefighters show their support for Senator Barbara Boxer.

Elections for senators always draw a lot of interest. Political groups everywhere try to influence close Senate elections by donating money or volunteers. Of course, you have to live in, say, Oklahoma to vote for Oklahoma's senator. But money helps win elections. The party in charge of the Senate can get a lot more done than the minority party. So helping elect your party's candidate in an election on the other side of the country could mean that more laws you agree with may be passed.

THE FILIBUSTER IS ONE OF THE SENATE'S MOST FAMOUS STRATEGIES. UNDER Senate rules, a senator can speak on any topic as long as he or she pleases. A senator will do this to delay a vote on a bill. This action is called a filibuster. If a senator knows he is on the losing side of a vote, he might filibuster to prevent the bill from ever getting voted on at all.

Until 1917, a senator could filibuster until he was hoarse. But that year, the Senate made a rule saying two-thirds of the senators voting could stop a filibuster. This is called a cloture vote. Through the years, the percentage needed for cloture has changed, but the rule remains. If the cloture vote passes, debate is limited to 30 hours and any single senator can speak only one hour.

Filibusters sometimes crop up during important votes. The debate on the Treaty of Versailles, the agreement ending World War I (1914–1918), was so bitter that the Senate voted for cloture for the first time. During the 1950s and 1960s, southern senators sometimes used the filibuster to defeat civil rights laws. South Carolina's Strom Thurmond's (right) 24-hour, 18-minute filibuster against the Civil Rights Act of 1957 still holds the record for the longest filibuster.

Chapter FOUR

Congress at Work

THE AVERAGE CITIZEN DOESN'T GET TO VOTE ON BILLS in Congress. But that doesn't mean you can't influence how senators and representatives vote.

Politicians pay a lot of attention to group action. Groups have the volunteers and votes politicians need to get elected. Politically active groups work to pass new legislation, change existing laws, or alter bills that are being considered. Two types of groups are very good at getting—and keeping—a congressman's attention.

Political Action Committees, or PACs, raise and donate money to candidates. Businesses and labor unions form corporate PACs. These PACS tend to be big. They have lots of money to give to candidates. A second kind of

Vice President Dick Cheney speaks at a fundraiser for Representative Jim Gerlach. Members of Congress need to raise money to pay for their election campaigns.

PAC organizes around a single issue or cause. With a little paperwork and at least $1,000 in donations, any group of citizens can become a PAC.

Lobbies also have great influence. A lobby is a group with a specific set of interests that spends time and money making sure legislators hear their opinions. Now more than ever, lobbies are big players in Washington, D.C. Big lobbies include the American Association of Retired Persons (AARP) and the National Rifle Association (NRA).

Lobbies sometimes write new legislation for members of Congress to submit. But you don't need to be a professional lobbying group to write a new law. Anyone can write a bill. Just read an existing bill and use its format to write the bill you have in mind. By submitting your idea for a bill in legal language, you save a congressperson's staff the trouble of having to write it up.

If you want to get your bill passed, you'll have to be patient. There's a lot going on in Congress. Pushing a piece of legislation through both houses takes years.

Let's say you convince your House representative to submit a bill for you. Once your bill is put in proper form, the Clerk of the House gives it a title and number. The Speaker of the House then assigns the bill to a committee. The assignment depends on what the bill concerns. If your bill creates a wildlife refuge, for instance, it would probably go to the

Members of the Senate Appropriations Subcommittee on Labor, Health and Human Services, and Education listen to testimony regarding a bill. Most of the work of the Senate takes place in subcommittees.

Committee on Resources. Sometimes two committees consider a bill, if it concerns two areas.

The committee chairman has the right to refuse to discuss any piece of legislation. If for any reason he doesn't like your bill, he can simply refuse to put it on the schedule. This means the bill will never be considered—it is dead.

Otherwise, the chairman sends it to a subcommittee. The subcommittee is an even smaller group that specializes in a certain area. The members of the subcommittee do most of the work. The subcommittee holds hearings to gather information from experts and other interested people.

After holding hearings, the subcommittee makes changes to the bill. Sometimes it's a word or two, sometimes a lot more. Finally, the subcommittee recommends the bill be passed, doesn't recommend it but puts it up for a vote, or throws it out.

If it's not thrown out, the bill then goes back to the full committee. Other committee members then make their own changes. At last, the bill is sent to the full House for a vote.

If your bill passes in the House, then it goes to the Senate. There it's sent to a Senate committee and the process starts all over again! If the bill also passes the Senate, it is still not done. The president can undo all of the work by vetoing the bill.

If the president signs it, though, the bill becomes law. During the next election, your representative can point to the new law and say, "Vote for me because of this fantastic new wildlife refuge." He gets applause. You get the satisfaction of knowing you've helped your fellow citizens. You've also taken part in a process that goes back—rule by rule, bill by bill—to the birth of the United States.

The women and men in Congress do a lot of work behind the scenes and in committees. But when it comes down to it, the public mostly notices only one thing: How did they vote?

When deciding how to vote, members of Congress face intense pressure. Consider the bill proposing a wildlife refuge. A congresswoman voting on it has to weigh many things. She might be under pressure from her party's leaders to vote a certain way, because the party as a whole is taking a stand on the environment. An environmental PAC that wants the refuge in order to protect an endangered species of duck might be lobbying hard. Perhaps the congress-

27

woman made a campaign promise to oppose a new wildlife refuge because it would prevent a factory from being built nearby, costing jobs in her district.

The congresswoman might also have a deep personal belief that it's a great—or terrible—idea. So how does she vote? Making a decision in the face of all that is the congresswoman's job. If she makes the wrong choice, though, she's the one who pays on Election Day.

Voting Your Conscience

ONE OF THE HARDEST QUESTIONS FOR A CONGRESSPERSON IS, SHOULD I VOTE for what I believe, or should I vote for what my constituents want? This question is especially dangerous for House members because they face voters every two years. An unpopular vote is likely to be on people's minds at election time.

"Voting your conscience," or voting for what you believe in, can be especially hard if the legislation is important or about an emotional issue. But, as one former House member put it, "That's what we get paid for."

Jeannette Rankin was one of the most famous examples of a person who voted her conscience. Rankin was the first woman elected to the House. She was also a committed pacifist—she didn't believe in war. After the Japanese attacked Pearl Harbor, Hawaii, in 1941, the entire U.S. Congress voted to declare war—except for Rankin. Rankin refused to vote for any war, even if it cost her a seat in the House.

1787 On September 17, the Constitutional Convention approves the Constitution.

1788 The U.S. Constitution takes effect when the ninth state, New Hampshire, approves it on June 21.

1789 The 65 members of the new House of Representatives and the 22 members of the Senate meet for the first time in New York.

1793 Construction of the Capitol building begins in Washington, D.C.

1795 The Senate begins meeting in public.

1812 Massachusetts governor Elbridge Gerry approves a "gerrymandered" map of congressional districts in his state.

1816 The Senate sets up the committee system for dealing with legislation.

1868 On February 24, President Andrew Johnson becomes the first president impeached (accused of a crime) by the House; the Senate acquits him of all charges on May 16.

1911 A law passes setting the number of House members at 435.

1913 The Seventeenth Amendment allows voters to directly elect members of the Senate.

1917 The Senate passes the cloture rule.

1941 On December 8, Jeannette Rankin is the only member of Congress to vote against war with Japan.

1957 Senator Strom Thurmond of South Carolina delivers the longest filibuster in Senate history (24 hours, 18 minutes), arguing against a civil rights bill.

1979 C-Span, a cable TV channel, begins broadcasting the House of Representatives live.

1998 President Bill Clinton becomes the second president impeached by the House; the Senate acquits him in 1999.

Glossary TERMS

amendment (uh-MEND-munt)
An amendment is a change to the Constitution. The Nineteenth Amendment guaranteed women the right to vote.

committees (ku-MI-teez)
Committees are groups of people working together. In Congress, committees deal with legislation in specific subject areas.

compromise (KOM-pruh-mize)
A compromise is a settlement in which each side gets part of what it wants. Roger Sherman's compromise at the Constitutional Convention created the two houses of Congress.

constituents (kun-STI-chu-uhnts)
Constituents are people who live in an electoral district. Representatives sometimes do favors for their constituents.

constitution (kon-stuh-TOO-shun)
A constitution is a document outlining the structure and basic laws of a government. The U.S. Constitution was written in 1787.

delegates (DE-li-guts)
Delegates are people who represent other people at a meeting. Delegates from 12 states gathered in Philadelphia to write the constitution.

democracy (di-MAH-kruh-see)
In a democracy, the citizens elect the members of a government. The United States is a democracy.

legislation (le-jus-LAY-shun)
Legislation is a rule or law that is put up for a vote by a government. Congress writes and passes new legislation.

legislature (LE-jus-lay-chur)
A legislature is a group that makes laws. Congress is the legislature of the U.S. government.

majority (mah-JOR-uh-tee)
In politics, to have a majority means to have the most votes or the most members in a government body. The Speaker of the House of Representatives is a member of the majority party. The opposite of a majority is a minority.

revenues (RE-vu-newz)
Revenues are taxes and other money collected by the government. Congress decides how to spend the U.S. government revenues.

veto (VEE-tow)
To veto is to reject. The president can veto legislation passed by Congress.

For Further INFORMATION

Books

Donovan, Sandra. *Running for Office: A Look at Political Campaigns.* Minneapolis: Lerner Publications, 2004.

Gutman, Dan. *Landslide! A Kid's Guide to the U.S. Elections.* New York: Aladdin Paperbacks, 2000.

Partner, Daniel. *The House of Representatives.* Philadelphia: Chelsea House, 2000.

Sobel, Syl, and Pam Tanzey (illustrator). *How the U.S. Government Works.* Hauppauge, N.Y.: Barron's, 1999.

Web sites

Visit our home page for lots of links about the U.S. Congress:
http://www.childsworld.com/links.html

Note to Parents, Teachers, and Librarians:
We routinely verify our Web links to make sure they're safe, active sites—so encourage your readers to check them out!

Places to Visit or Contact

The National Archives Building
To see the U.S. Constitution and learn more about this important document
700 Pennsylvania Avenue NW
Washington, DC 20408
866/272-6272

The U.S. Capitol
To see the building where the U.S. Congress meets
First Street SW and Independence Avenue
Washington, DC
202/225-6827

31

Index

About the Author

KEVIN CUNNINGHAM IS AN AUTHOR AND TRAVEL WRITER. HE studied journalism and history at the University of Illinois at Urbana. His other books include *Condoleezza Rice: Educator and Presidential Adviser, Power to the People: How We Elect the President and Other Officials,* and *The Declaration of Independence.* He lives in Chicago.

DATE			